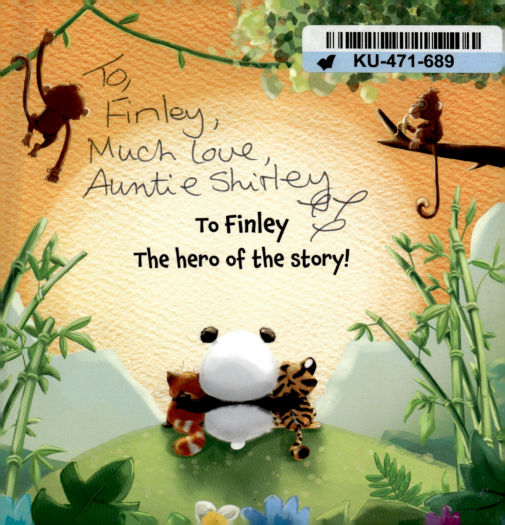

To **Finley**

The hero of the story!

Finley Panda and his friends are playing their best-loved game of roly poly.

It is lots of fun and much better than walking.

4

Down and down,

round and round they roll.

Bopping into each other

and bouncing off trees and bushes,

Pandas are so fluffy they never get hurt.

5

Suddenly –
SPLASH!

they roll into an unexpected puddle of water.
Where has it come from? It hasn't been raining!

As they shake the water from their fur,

Finley can see that the nearby river has burst its banks and he wonders why.

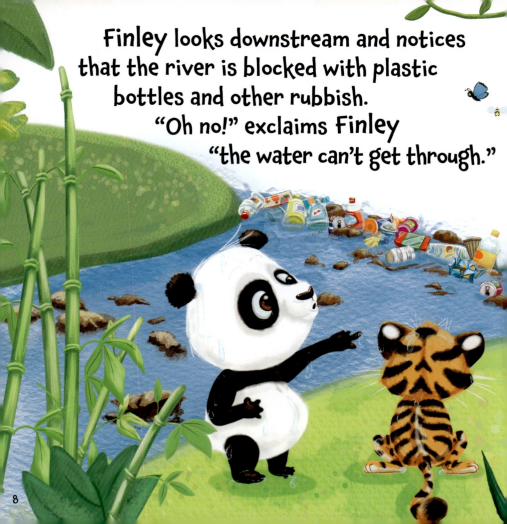

Finley looks downstream and notices that the river is blocked with plastic bottles and other rubbish.
"Oh no!" exclaims Finley "the water can't get through."

"We will have
to remove the rubbish,
or more of the jungle could
be flooded. That would be a
disaster for our friends and
food supply." says Finley.
But how?

Finley looks around
and sees his friend
Tumble is eating
some bamboo...

...and this
gives him
an idea.

10

Finley asks Tumble to chomp down two long lengths of bamboo,

while he tears off strips from another piece and cleverly twists the strips into a net.

Working together the friends make an amazing makeshift bridge.

They wonder how to get it across the water.

"I know" says the tallest stretchiest monkey, waggling his floppy hands, "I can swing across!"

Using an extra long vine and taking an extra big leap...

...the monkey swings safely to the other side, landing like an acrobat.

Bit by bit, Finley and his friends push the bamboo bridge across to him. The monkey stretches out his long arms and grabs the bridge, then using some vines he ties the bamboo bridge tightly to a nearby tree.

13

Finley carefully shimmies out onto the bridge.
Being a bear, he's not
scared of climbing.

Just as he reaches the middle he loses
his grip and starts to slip!

Luckily he manages to hang on with his strong legs and sharp claws. Dangling upside down, he sees that he is close to the rubbish swirling in the water below.

Clinging on to the bridge, Finley begins scooping up the nasty rubbish with the net.

15

The other jungle creatures all want to help, so Finley passes the rubbish filled net to a monkey...

...who then gives it to the red panda...

16

...who finally hands it to the tiger!

The tiger empties the rubbish into one big pile.
"Why don't we call ourselves the Eco Crew,
as we are doing such a good job."
says the tiger. "That is a great idea."
says Finley.

Finally, the last piece of rubbish is collected...

...and the river runs freely again. HOORAY!

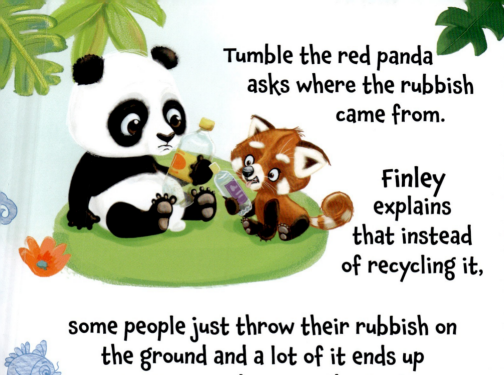

Tumble the red panda asks where the rubbish came from.

Finley explains that instead of recycling it,

some people just throw their rubbish on the ground and a lot of it ends up in rivers and even in the SEA!

"That is terrible," says the red panda.
"We should remind everyone that –
If everybody does their bit
the planet will be fighting fit."

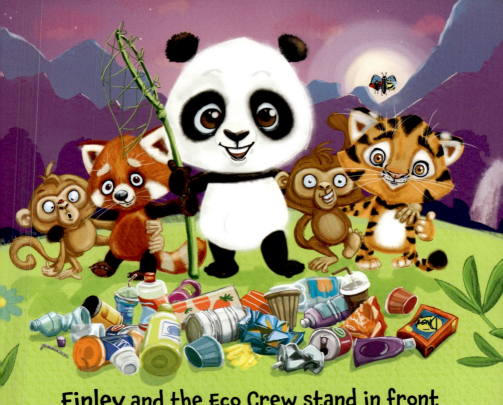

Finley and the Eco Crew stand in front
of the big pile of rubbish, happy with
doing their bit to help.

The end

THE
TEAPOT

THE

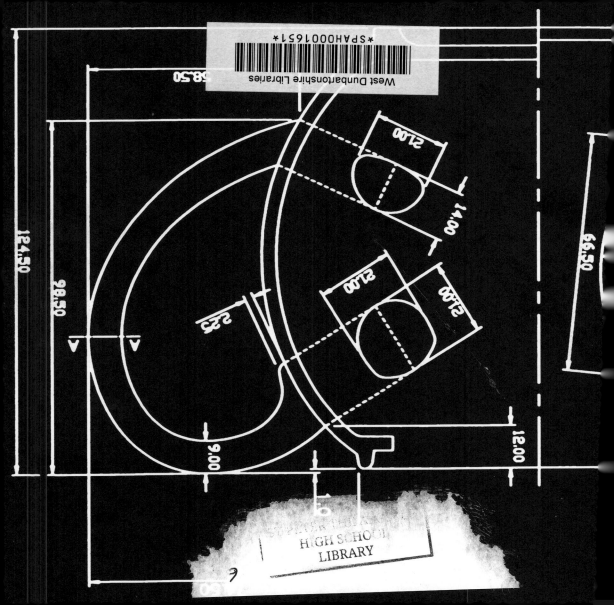

TEAPOT

AN APPRECIATION

AURUM PRESS

GUY JULIER ◉ PHOTOGRAPHS BY GUY RYECART

First published in Great Britain 1998 by
Aurum Press Limited
25 Bedford Avenue
London WC1B 2AT

A catalogue record for this book is
available from the British Library

ISBN 1 85410 597 3

This book was conceived,
designed and produced by
THE IVY PRESS LIMITED
2/3 St Andrews Place
Lewes, East Sussex
BN7 1UP

Art Director: *Peter Bridgewater*
Editorial Director: *Sophie Collins*
Managing Editor: *Anne Townley*
Project Editor: *Caroline Earle*
Editor: *Julie Whitaker*
Designer: *Ron Bryant-Funnell*
Photography: *Guy Ryecart*

Printed and bound in China

Throughout this book the dimensions of
the objects are given in imperial and
metric measurements; height and width
are expressed by H and W.

22

13

23

15

25

11

24

15

29

17

20

23

30

29

31

26

20

16

28

19

14

12

10

27

24

17

21

25

27

18

16

11

14

14

19

13

28

Introduction

Few modern products are subjected to such exhaustive consumer scrutiny as the teapot. The dangers of dribbling on starched white teacloths or vulnerable limbs; the weight-to-volume balance, which changes on pouring; the appropriateness of materials and shape to provide the perfect cuppa – all present the designer with an exacting creative task.

This is even before the teapot's symbolic or emblematic values are examined. Through its constant re-use, the teapot comes to signify a social ritual. But more literally, the teapot takes centre stage in a social event by becoming a source of conversation. Its role reaches far beyond the material clutter of our everyday lives.

None the less, despite various attempts, few classic teapots of lasting effect have been designed. From the teapot's first European appearance in the early 18th century, its form and decoration changed with startling

Cadbury Typhoo Disposable
Henry Dudzik
1984

regularity. As the hardware for a luxury drink, it became an object of high fashion in the courts and country houses of England.

Tea and teasets were first imported from China but, lacking the technical skills to reproduce the high standards of porcelain-making to be found in the Far East, the British potteries soon set about creating their own genre of teapot. Hence the novelty

Tournée
Queensbury-Hunt
1989

teapot was established. Themes came and went with changing fashions: vegetable, animal or human forms appeared; important political events or technological advances of the time were also featured. Their idiosyncrasies and enormous variety have encouraged an energetic and popular collectors' market. Indeed, in the later 20th century several smaller-scale manufacturers have survived by specializing in this genre.

The turn of the 20th century saw a flourish of gadget teapots on both sides of the Atlantic. With the growth of mass consumption, the rapidly increasing competition for market share between a large number of manufacturers spawned some ingenious and bizarre products for satiating the public's diverse demands for tea-making hardware.

Jemima
Otaigiri/Fitz and Floyd
1985

Bandalasta
Arnold Brookes, 1927

Meanwhile, in the wake of the influential late-19th-century design-reformers such as Henry Cole, John Ruskin and William Morris, a more serious teapot type was established. The whimsical novelty teapots, judged as shoddy and ephemeral, were countered by more austere and functional looking forms. In their quest for the perfect teapot, British advocates of the Modern Movement often dragged up the most ordinary looking traditional pieces, such as the ubiquitous Brown Betty, and held them aloft as the ultimate in formal purism and practicality. Equally, Modernists across continental Europe rose to a new challenge to create the archetypal teapot during the inter-war years. Indeed, to this day, the teapot has quietly stood alongside the chair as a standard design-and-making exercise in decorative arts academies and for the establishment of a professional's kudos as a practitioner of high design.

Japanese teapot
Ray Finch, 1959

As a basis for artistic expression and the perfecting of handiwork, the teapot has also maintained a prime position amongst studio-craftspeople. In the earlier 20th century this was dominated by a mystical mixture of Japanese perfectionism and medieval revivalism, as professed by Bernard Leach and Michael Cardew and evidenced by a plethora of muddy brown productions. However, in the 1970s this heavy aesthetic was broken when studio-craft became increasingly experimental and sculptural in conception. Every unwritten functional, colouristic, ergonomic and commercial rule surrounding the teapot has subsequently been broken.

In recent, Postmodern times the categories of novelty, gadget, high-design and studio-craft teapots have frequently converged. The Italian company Alessi has been instrumental in drawing a craft ethic into the volume production of high-design teaware whilst embuing its products with playful qualities. Meanwhile, many historical designs, such as those of Marianne Brandt or Clarice Cliff, have been revived. The teapot is also divesting itself of its strongly British connotations, as the promotion of tea as a healthier alternative to coffee – particularly in Scandinavia and the USA – is giving the product a new international impetus. The teapot is currently the object of many conversations in many languages.

Porcelain teapot
Lubomir Tomaszewski, 1950s

SILVER-PLATED BRASS, 1900. H7.5 X W12IN / H19 X W30.5CM

SILVER TEAPOT

PAUL FOLLOT/CHRISTOFLE

Designed at the height of the French Art Nouveau style, this exuberant piece demonstrates that its extreme whiplash effects were not confined to architectural metalwork or jewellery. The young Paul Follot included an exaggerated spout and handle, which are not only highly voguish for the teapot's time but also make it an excellent pourer.

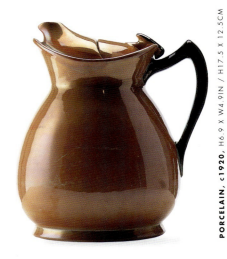

CHAMELEON

**R. C. JOHNSON /
GEORGE CLEWS & CO. LTD**

Manufactured with a huge variety of applied decorative effects, from mock silver to floral patterns, the Chameleon became extremely popular in tea houses during the inter-war years. Originally designed for the Cunard shipping line, the cuboid teapot would not tip over on the high seas. This stylish object was, however, a recalcitrant dribbler.

COSY

**POUNTNEY & CO. LTD
(PATENTED BY ABRAM ALLWARE LTD)**

Vigorously marketed as the perfect dripless teapot, the Cosy was patented in 26 countries. Lacking a spout, tea collected in an upper chamber before being poured out. It was subjected to a wide variety of applied decorations. The product also boasted greater ease of cleaning for the hygiene-conscious, and, for the nervous, a lid that did not slip off.

SILVER, WOOD, 1925

H3.4 X W6.8IN / H8.5 X W17CM

SILVER TEAPOT

JEAN E. PUIFORCAT/PUIFORCAT

Jean E. Puiforcat was a principal exponent of 1920s Art Deco in dinnerware. The geometric styling of this teapot allows classicism to be combined with a hint of modernity. The use of wood means that the heat from the pot is not conducted to the handle, while the lid features the inlaid initials of its first owner.

CORNISH BLUE

T.G. GREEN & CO. LTD
RESTYLED BY JUDITH ONIONS

Like the Brown Betty, T. G. Green's Cornish Blue kitchenware was enthusiastically commended in the 1920s by British design reformers for its functionality and simple abstract decoration. The blue and white stripes derive from 19th-century craft-made pottery. Judith Onions's 1960s restyling of the form, which gives it a more geometric feel, was the subject of much controversy amongst die-hard collectors, who preferred its original, more bulbous style.

BANDALASTA

ARNOLD BROOKES /
BROOKES AND ADAMS

Manufactured in urea thiourea formaldehyde – tradename Bandalasta – this plastic teapot was marketed as part of a picnicware set. Clearly such innovative use of plastic had advantages over more traditional materials for such purposes, but it was prone to chipping. The combination of bright colouring and marbled effect, somewhat ahead of its time, did not achieve wide public approbation, and by 1932 Brookes and Adams had switched to plainer designs.

EARTHENWARE, c1930, H7 X W9.8IN / H17.5 X W24.5CM

BURG GIEBICHENSTEIN

MARGARIT FRIEDLANDER / STAATLICHT PORZELLAN- MANUFAKTUR

In Germany in the 1920s and early 1930s, several industrial ceramics designers, including Hermann Gretsch, Wilhelm Wagenfeld and Margarit Friedlander, strove to design a standard form for tea and coffee services for the state porcelain manufactories. The clean lines of this Friedlander teapot are the clear evidence of her Bauhaus training.

DOUBLE-DECKER

Whilst the overall form mimics that of a standard teapot, the upper and lower sections are separated. The lower part contained hot water, which kept the upper tea-chamber warm and could be used for re-fills. Commercial competition was rife in the early 20th century, and many such brewing gadgets appeared to claim their market niche.

PORCELAIN, 1931, H5 X W8.2IN / H12.5 X W20.5CM

KESTREL
SUSIE COOPER/WOOD AND SONS LTD

Produced into the 1950s and reintroduced by Wedgwood in 1988, the Kestrel's form echoes the sophisticated Modernist lines of 1930s architecture, while its bird-like detailing lends a contemporary feel to the object. The formal clarity of the Kestrel makes it adaptable to different decorations, from freehand painting to lithography. This reflects Susie Cooper's deep understanding of the needs of decoration alongside the creation of form.

EARTHENWARE, 1932,
H5 X W7IN / H12.5 X W17.5CM

EARTHENWARE WITH HANDPAINTED DECORATION, 1932
H4.6 X W7.4IN / H11.5 X W18.5CM

ODILON (A.K.A. CONICAL)
CLARICE CLIFF/NEWPORT POTTERY CO. LTD

Clarice Cliff's celebrated Bizarre range of tableware met stiff resistance when it was first produced. First, supporters of Modernism saw her application of rich colours and strong forms as superficial. In addition, contemporary retailers thought her Art Deco-inspired designs were too advanced. Cliff had already identified a healthy market for progressive design at reasonable prices, though. Indeed, demand for this teapot often outstripped supply.

TRANSPARENT TEAPOT

WILHELM WAGENFELD / JANAER GLASWERK SCHOTT UND GENOSSEN

The transparent teapot is something of a rarity. Manufactured from the same heat-resistant glass that was used for test-tubes, it featured a cylindrical infuser. This allowed the user to judge the strength of tea visually and then remove the tea leaves. However, it is an idea that has never really caught on. Tea-makers, it seems, prefer their trade to be a form of craft-knowledge rather than scientific analysis.

PIQUOT WARE

ALFRED EDWARD BURRAGE / BURRAGE & BOYD

Robustly elegant, this product was intended for more informal entertaining: it is shiny but not too posh! Aluminium had previously been confined to kitchenware. Here it successfully makes the transition to the table. This use of aluminium paved the way for the popular acceptance of stainless steel after World War II.

RACING CAR

SADLER & SONS LTD

The 1930s saw a boom decade for novelty teapots. The Racing Car sold in its thousands, its popularity perhaps reflecting the ascendance of motor transport during that decade. The teapot's registration – OKT42 – evokes the halcyon days of motoring for pleasure and romance. Some versions included a trailer for a sugar-bowl.

STAINLESS STEEL; BAKELITE HANDLE AND KNOB, 1945, H6 X W5IN / H15 X W12.7CM

BOMBE

CARLO ALESSI/ALESSI

As a design-led manufacturer of tableware, Alessi was a key player in the re-invigoration of Italian material culture in the postwar period. The object's robust form is carried by the Roman-amphora-like body, whilst the finial adds a playful detail. Such quirky classicism has become a clear feature of Italian design.

EARTHENWARE,

1930s,

H4.4 X W9IN

H11 X W23CM

PRIDE

DAVID MELLOR/ELKINGTONS

NICKEL ELECTROPLATED WITH

Whilst many postwar designers have created highly complex forms, treating the teapot as a formal exercise to demand the viewer's attention, Mellor has consistently sought a less obstrusive, yet more lasting, style. Despite its highly classical roots in 18th-century silverware, the Pride mixes precious and non-precious materials, making it more accessible to a middle market.

SILVER; CELLULOID HANDLE AND FINIAL, 1957
H5 X W9.4IN / H12.7 X W24CM

STONEWARE, 1959,
H9.4 X W8IN / H24 X W20CM

JAPANESE TEAPOT

RAY FINCH

The traditional Japanese teapot was widely adopted by the so-called brown-mug school of British potters as a standard form in the mid-20th century. This was combined with surface treatment more akin to medieval English ceramics. Although a quaint idea, the positioning and lack of rigidity of the bamboo handle make the pot difficult to pour whilst sitting at a table.

TAC1

WALTER GROPIUS AND LOUIS MCMILLEN/ROSENTHAL

As a founder of the Bauhaus, and arch champion of Modernism, Walter Gropius was well known for classical restraint in his architectural projects. This product stays within the typically clean lines that are a hallmark of Rosenthal's porcelain. A glimpse of a more expressive nature is allowed in the teapot's spout, however.

METAL TEAPOT

WMF

This is an unusual teapot by Germany's best-known tableware manufacturer. Its correctness of form suggests the inheritance of pre-war Rationalism, while its slightly bulbous proportions in the spout and vessel acknowledge a more contemporary organic feel. The handle is treated with a plastic covering – itself evidence of the growing acceptance of plastic at the table – thus cutting down heat conduction.

ELECTROPLATED METAL, 1950s,
H4.2 X W8.8IN / H10.5 X W22CM

PORCELAIN, 1962, H6 X W7.7IN / H15 X W19.5CM

PORCELAIN TEAPOT

LUBOMIR TOMASZEWSKI/ CMIELÓW

The dazzling colour, decoration and curvilinear asymmetry of this piece are testimony to the little-appreciated fact that much design in the more liberal years of post-Stalinist Eastern Europe underwent significant modernization. Cmielów and the Czech firm Royal Dux produced extravagant creations that pushed the European fashion for organic shapes even further.

STAINLESS STEEL; CELLULOID HANDLE, 1967, H5.2 X W9.4IN / H13 X W23.5CM

CYLINDA LINE

ARNE JACOBSEN /
A. S. STELTON

Based on the standard dimensions of stainless steel tubing, the Cylinda Line retains a utilitarian authority that is refined by the sleek contours of Danish Modernism. Its elongated spout is a typical detail of much 20th-century Scandinavian design, charging its sobriety with a more sensuous or even sexual quality.

EARTHENWARE, EARLY 1970s, H8 X W9.4IN / H20.5 X W24CM

TELEVISION

SOUTH WEST CERAMICS FOR TEA COUNCIL

A deliciously irreverent commentary on the accommodation of one form of popular culture by another, in that the object reminds us that the television commercial break also serves as a tea break. The Television is an unusual novelty teapot when we consider that so many of this type refer to anything but tea drinking.

CAMEL
CARLTON WARE

Whilst themes for the novelty teapot came and went – reflecting our changing culture – it is reassuring to see the return of the camel to the tea service. This animal was first seen on the teapot in the mid-18th century. Carlton Ware specialized in novelty teapots and has been responsible for the revival of many themes.

EARTHENWARE, EARLY 1970s, H6.9 X W5.9IN / H17.5 X W15CM

PORCELAIN, 1974, H4.4 X W9.6IN / H11 X W24.5CM

DROP
LUIGI COLANI/ROSENTHAL

Colani has applied his stridently biomorphic style to trains, motorbikes, cameras and... teapots. Like Gropius's TAC1, Rosenthal produced this in very limited numbers. Despite its highly exaggerated streamlining – owing something to Colani's interest in undersea forms – its smooth lines bestow a timeless modernity to the object.

EARTHENWARE, 1976,
H7 X W 7IN / H17.5 X W17.5CM

SILVER, EBONY, GLASS, 1980,
H7.5 X W8.3IN / H19 X W21CM

WALKING TEAPOT

ROGER MICHELL AND DANKA NAPIORKOWSHA / CARLTON WARE

Conceived as a craft piece, this characterful teapot soon found its way into high-volume production in the 1980s. Several stances were available. The mass manufacture of novelty teapots such as this enabled makers to cash in on the commercially more dependable gift market in recessionary times.

ORANDA

OSCAR TUSQUETS / ALESSI

Tusquets's submission to the Alessi's '11 Architects Design Teapots Project' was the only one not to attempt micro-architecture but, instead, to treat the teapot in its own terms. It is also the only teapot from this project that pours well and sold consistently throughout the 1980s.

SILVER; EBONY HANDLE, 1980,
H6 X W6IN / H15 X W15CM

PLASTIC, 1984, H4 X W5 IN / H10 X W12.5CM

SILVER TEAPOT

ROBERT VENTURI/ALESSI

Venturi's design for the celebrated Alessi 'Tea and Coffee Piazza' Project took the banality of the contemporary urban landscape as its theme. In the teapot he combined the proportions of classical architecture in form with a kitsch graphic element in decoration. The implicit cultural commentary recreates the humble teapot as micro-meta-architecture.

CADBURY TYPHOO DISPOSABLE

HENRY DUDZIK/ MARDON ILLINGWORTH FOR CADBURY TYPHOO

Conceived to add more dignity to take away tea, this disposable teapot allowed you to pour your own. It features several design innovations: the lid is removable for those who prefer to stir their tea; the spout has a non-drip tip, while tea is poured by tearing back a tab at a deliberately weak spot. Small wonder that many users found it too attractive and functional to throw away.

EARTHENWARE,
1985,
H4IN / H10CM

JEMIMA

OTAIGIRI COMMISSIONED / MARKETED BY FITZ AND FLOYD

There is a peculiar irony in the existence of this product, and many others manufactured in the Far East for the Western market since the 1980s. English potters developed the novelty teapot concept in the early 18th century, unable as they were to compete with the Chinese and Japanese in the production of high-quality porcelain. Globalization has seen the story of the novelty teapot come almost full-circle!

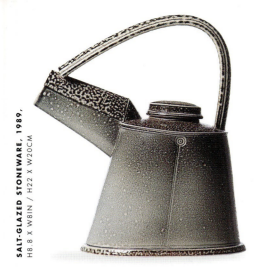

SALT-GLAZED STONEWARE, 1989,
H8.8 X W8IN / H22 X W20CM

EARTHENWARE, 1989,
H5.6 X W9.6IN / H14 X W24.5CM

STONEWARE TEAPOT

WALTER KEELER

Keeler has dismantled the basic attributes of the teapot – handle, spout and vessel – and reconstructed it in an intriguing and ingenious way. However, whilst many contemporary craftspeople look to deconstruct everyday objects to the point of dysfunction, this piece pours perfectly.

TOURNÉE

QUEENSBURY HUNT

Recognizing that the archetype of any tableware product has already been resolved, Queensbury Hunt saw their role as the fine tuners of conventional forms. The idiosyncratic twist awarded here to the finial and handle gives this teapot a much more contemporary and distinctive effect. Design success in many late 20th-century products depends on the details.

BOROSILICATE GLASS,
STAINLESS STEEL,
POLYPROPYLENE, 1992,
H5 X W5.7IN /
H12.5 X W14.5CM

PORCELAIN, ALUMINIUM, STAINLESS STEEL,
1994, H8.8 X W7.2IN / H22 X W18CM

TEAPOT 2000

CARSTEN JORGENSEN/BODUM

A development from the Wagenfeld teapot, the perforated central column contains the tea leaves. The plunger is pushed down and confines the leaves to the bottom, hence stopping the infusion at the desired moment. Style and science thus unite to create the perfect cup of tea.

TI TANG

PHILIPPE STARCK/ALESSI

Philippe Starck, renowned designer of lemon-squeezers that splash and kettles that splutter, has turned just about every household appliance into a lifestyle object of contemplation. This teapot illustrates his famously precarious organic style. The added conceit here is that the teapot's instability encourages the tea leaves to circulate more freely, apparently facilitating a better brew.

EARTHENWARE WITH EN GLAZE ENAMEL
DECORATION, 1994
H 6.6 X W 13.4IN / H16.5 X W33.5CM

COILED TEAPOT

CAROL MCNICOLL

Much late 20th-century studio-craft used just about any everyday object as a vehicle for artistic expression. Here, brightly coloured and wittily unexpected forms and decoration are explored, almost in deliberate contrast to the sombre functionality of the earlier studio pottery of Cardew and Leach. As in many of McNicoll's works, weaving and knotting are featured.

BROWN BETTY

CERACRAFT, ASCOT AND RIDGWAY

The origins of its name are unclear, but the homely, rich associations of the words Brown Betty have stuck. Despite its very traditional design, and its self-consciously nostalgic branding (it was sold as Genuine Old English Brownware), this teapot was hailed by design reformers in the 1920s for its uncompromising form and efficiency as both brewer and pourer.

EARTHENWARE, 1996, H6.4 X W10IN / H16 X W25CM

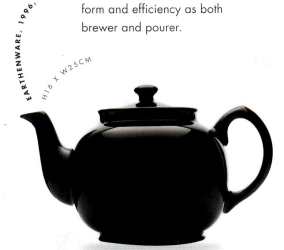

HAND

JILL CROWLEY

The rough and ready Hand is one of the most extreme studio-craft considerations of the novelty teapot. Crowley had explored the hand theme in sculptural pieces for several years, but had also produced several eccentric designs, including a herd of teapots in 1973. Logically, the thumb provides the spout.

OXIDIZED STONEWARE, 1996, H12.4 X W13.6IN / H31 X W34CM

PORCELAIN TEAPOT

NICHOLAS HOMOKY

PORCELAIN, 1997, H6.3 X W8.3IN / H16 X W21CM

The non-functional basic form of this teapot is juxtaposed with a standard-looking spout. Homoky exploits the limited space of the object's surface to the full, using inlay to produce clean lines that suggest, rather than illustrate, household objects. In this way, a series of tensions are built up through the piece.

ACKNOWLEDGEMENTS

The publishers would particularly like to thank the
following for loan of teapots:

Betjeman & Barton, Brighton: pages 2-3,
29 (right)
Bramah Tea and Coffee Museum, London:
11 (right), 22, 23 (left), 26, 28 (left)
Capricorn, Eastbourne: 13 (left)
Jill Crowley: 30
Design Museum: 16 (right), 21, 32 (Private
Collection courtesy of Design Museum); 14 (right),
23 (right), 18, 28 (right) (Collection of Design Museum)
Nicholas Homoky: 31
John Jesse: 1, 9, 10, 12, 13 (right), 20
Guy Julier: 11(left)
Sylvia Katz: 6, 25 (right)
Walter Keeler: 27 (left)
Robin Levien: 7, 27 (right)
Pavilion Museum, Brighton: 15 (right),
19 (right)
Teapot World, Conway: 8, 14 (left),
15 (left), 16 (left), 17 (left), 19 (left), 24 (left)
Ed Wolf: page 29 (left)

The publishers wish to thank the following
for the use of pictures:
Alessi spa, Italy: 17 (right),
24 (right), 25 (left).

Endpapers: Kyomi designed by
Queensbury Hunt Levien

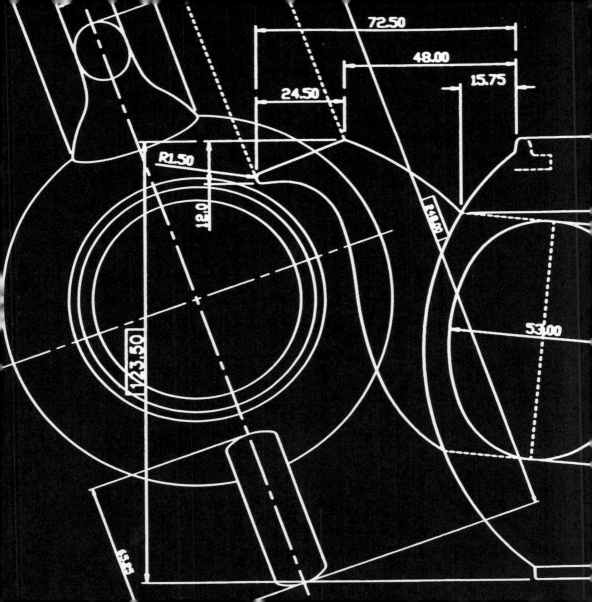

The end of Kate's bed was a lonely place.
Tiger the cat no longer slept there. Tiger died last winter,
so there were only Kate's two feet to keep each other company.

Now Kate woke to Full Summer with the sun pouring
over the back fence…

For Carolyn, Rosy and Sasha

First published 2001 by Walker Books Ltd
87 Vauxhall Walk, London SE11 5HJ

This edition published 2012

10 9 8 7 6 5 4 3 2 1

© 2001 Blackbird Design Pty Ltd

The right of Bob Graham to be identified
as author/illustrator of this work has been
asserted by him in accordance with the
Copyright, Designs and Patents Act 1988

This book has been typeset in Bulmer

Printed in China

British Library Cataloguing in
Publication Data:
a catalogue record for this book is
available from the British Library

ISBN 978-1-4063-4313-7

www.walker.co.uk

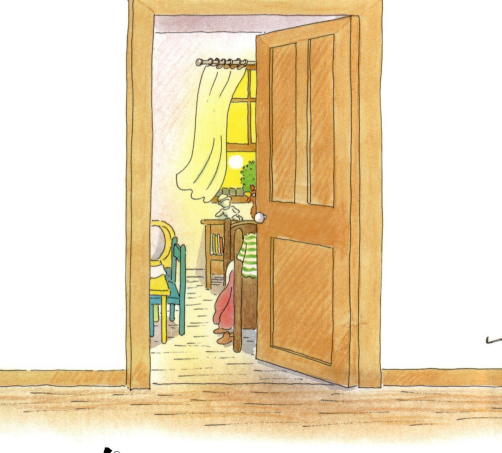

WALKER BOOKS
AND SUBSIDIARIES
LONDON · BOSTON · SYDNEY · AUCKLAND

"Let's Get a
PUP!"

BOB GRAHAM

"Let's get a pup!"

said Kate.

"What, a brand-new one?" said a
now wide-awake Mum.

"With the wrapping still on?" added
her breathless dad.

"Pups don't come wrapped," replied
Kate.

"I know they don't," said Dad.

"It's just a joke."

Mum looked in the paper.

"It must be small," said Kate.

"And cute," said Dad.

"And get all excited," said Kate.

"And run round in circles," said Dad.

"Hmm," said Mum. "LOOK!"

THE RESCUE CENTRE

The centre for dogs without a home
The centre for dogs all alone

With their breakfast uneaten,
they dressed and left
immediately.

At the Rescue Centre they found
plenty of dogs without a home,
and lots of dogs all alone.
They found …

big dogs, small dogs, sniffers and
sleepers, wire-haireds, short-haireds,
scratchers and leapers.

They found fighters and biters,
growlers and snarlers, short dogs,
dogs long and thin, and dogs with their
cheeks sucked in.

They also found happy dogs,
sad dogs, "take me" dogs, and
dogs who couldn't care less.

They saw smelly dogs, fat dogs,
lean and mean dogs, chew-it-up-
and-spit-it-out-at-you dogs,
and dogs like walking nightmares.

Then they saw …

Dave.

Dave was so excited
he came out sideways.
He barked twice,
water flew off his
tongue and he
turned a complete
circle in the air.

He was small.

He was cute.

He was brand-new.

Dave climbed right
over the top of Kate,
who briefly wore
him like a hat.

"He's all that we want," said Kate.

"All that we came for,"
  said Mum.

"We'll take him,"
  said Dad.

Then they saw …

Rosy.

And she saw them.
She was old and
grey and broad
as a table. It was
difficult for her to
get to her feet, but she
stood, it seemed, almost politely.
Her eyes watered, her ears went back
and she radiated Good Intention.

"My wish for you," said Dad, "is that you
could lie on someone's living-room floor."

"Or on their couch," said Mum.

"Or on someone's bed," said Kate.

Mum's voice shook.

"We would take them all if we could,
but what can we do?"

And with many a backward glance ...

they slowly walked away.

At home, Dave was everything
that a pup could be,
and more.

On his first night, he cried in his carton.

The next morning, Kate's mum and dad
received a good licking.
"Dave was crying last night, so he slept with me,"
said Kate. "But I didn't sleep…"
"Neither did I," said Dad. "I was wishing…"
"Neither did I," said Mum. "I was wishing…"

With their breakfast
once again uneaten,
they dressed and left
immediately.

At the Rescue Centre

Rosy was waiting for them.

"Let's get you home," said Dad.

Rosy was instantly at home.
Her broad heavy tail swept everything
off the low table.

"I've seen a dog
smelling a man,
but never a man
smelling a dog,"
said Kate's mum.
"She needs a bath,"
said Dad.

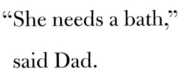

Now Dad's wish has come true.

Rosy is asleep on the living-room floor,

with Dave to keep her company.

Mum's wish has also come true.
Now Rosy and Dave are asleep
on the couch.

And what of Kate's wish?

Will it come true as well?

Yes.

Dave and Rosy *will* get to sleep
on someone's bed.

Kate puts her head on
Rosy's stomach. She hears
angry gurgles, squeaks and
plops, lonely corkscrew
sounds, and the pump,
pump, pump of Rosy's
heart, like a big hollow
engine room.

Kate's feet are no longer lonely under the blankets.
It seems like Dave and Rosy have always been there.
Their weight is comfortable and reliable, and will stop
Kate's bed floating away into the night.